KOALAS

Koala Magic for Kids

METRIC CONVERSIONS:

1 foot = .3048 meter
1 pound = .4536 kilogram

For Ashley and Matt Speer
With special thanks to Barbara Harold
                                     — Kathy Feeney

For a free color catalog describing Gareth Stevens Publishing's list of high-quality books and multimedia programs, call 1-800-542-2595 (USA) or 1-800-461-9120 (Canada). Gareth Stevens Publishing's Fax: 414-225-0377.

Library of Congress Cataloging-in-Publication Data

Feeney, Kathy, 1954-
    Koala magic for kids / by Kathy Feeney; illustrated by
John F. McGee.
        p. cm. (Animal magic for kids)
    "Based on the book, Koalas for kids . . . by Kathy Feeney" —
T.p. verso.
    Includes bibliographical references and index.
    Summary: Describes the physical characteristics, habits, and natural
environment of the koala, a nocturnal marsupial found only in Australia.
    ISBN 0-8368-2635-3 (lib. bdg.)
    1. Koala—Juvenile literature. [1. Koala.] I. McGee, John F., ill.
II. Title. III. Series.
QL737.M384F434   2000
599.2'5—dc21   99-053368

First published in this edition in
North America in 2000 by
Gareth Stevens Publishing
1555 North RiverCenter Drive, Suite 201
Milwaukee, WI 53212 USA

Based on the book, *Koalas for Kids*, text © 1999 by Kathy Feeney, with illustrations by John F. McGee. First published in the United States in 1999 by NorthWord Press, Inc., (Creative Publishing International), 5900 Green Oak Drive, Minnetonka, MN 55343. End matter © 2000 by Gareth Stevens, Inc.

Photographs © 1999: Erwin & Peggy Bauer: cover, 3, 12, 15, 16, 20, 26-27, 30, 43, back cover; John Shaw: 7, 11, 33, 42; Martin Withers/Dembinsky Photo Associates: 8; Inga Spence/Tom Stack & Associates: 19, 24, 36; Brian Parker/Tom Stack & Associates: 23; Ed Kanze/Dembinsky Photo Associates: 29; Dave Watts/Tom Stack & Associates: 34, 40; John Cancalosi/Tom Stack & Associates: 39; Art Wolfe: 46.

Printed in the United States of America

1 2 3 4 5 6 7 8 9 04 03 02 01 00

by Kathy Feeney

KOALAS

Koala Magic for Kids

Gareth Stevens Publishing
MILWAUKEE

AUSTRALIA

Some people think koalas look like cuddly toy teddy bears with their shiny brown eyes, fluffy round ears, and rubbery black noses. They are often called "koala bears." But koalas are not bears.

These amazing Australian mammals are actually related to the kangaroo. This means the koala is a marsupial (mar-SOO-pee-ul). A female marsupial carries her baby in a pouch on her belly. But unlike the kangaroo, the koala has a pouch that opens from the bottom, like an upside-down pocket.

Australia is the only place on Earth where koalas are found in the wild. Years ago they roamed throughout this island continent. But now koalas live only in the eucalyptus (yoo-kul-IP-tus) tree forests along Australia's eastern and southern coasts.

Koalas are nocturnal, which means they are mostly active at night. That is also when they do most of their feeding. The koala's favorite food is the leaves of eucalyptus trees.

Eucalyptus leaves are spear-shaped and contain mostly water. In the morning these leaves are also covered with dew. Koalas get so much water by just eating them that they rarely take a drink. Yet sometimes they will sip water from streams and rivers that run through their forest homes.

Native Australian people are called aborigines (ab-o-RIJ-uh-nees). When they first saw the koala, the aborigines thought the animal never ever drank water. So they gave it a special name. "Koala" is an aboriginal word meaning "no drink."

Koalas are hardly ever thirsty because they get water from eating eucalyptus leaves.

This koala easily balances on a branch high in a eucalyptus tree.

Koalas grow to be about 2 feet tall and can weigh from 10 to 30 pounds. They have white chins and white chests. They also have white fur on the underside of their forearms. The rest of their coat is either gray or brown.

Their coloring blends in well with the eucalyptus tree bark. The fur of their coat is thicker and longer on the back than on the belly.

Their spotted rump also creates a natural camouflage that helps them hide in the trees. Their ears look fluffy and are covered with long, white hair.

There are 3 species (SPEE-sees), or kinds, of koalas: the Victoria, the New South Wales, and the Queensland.

The Victoria and the New South Wales koalas live in the southern part of Australia where the weather is cool. The Victoria koala is the largest. The New South Wales is the middle size of the three kinds. Both of these southern koalas have thick fur to keep them warm. The color of their coat is brown.

The smallest koala is the Queensland. It is found in Australia's warmer northern region. Because of the warmer temperatures where it lives, it has short-haired fur. Its coat is a light shade of gray.

Koalas may look chubby, but underneath their fluffy fur, they are lean and muscular.

Their fur changes to adapt to the different temperatures in their environment. Woolly waterproof coats keep them warm in cold weather and dry in rain.

When the seasons change and the weather warms, they can shed some of their fur to stay cool. It's like the layers of clothing that skiers wear to stay comfortable on the slopes. If they get too warm, they can simply remove a layer of clothing.

A koala's fur is like a warm raincoat.

Koalas do not have a tail. Their rump is padded fur.

While most people need a pillow to sit on something hard, the koala's built-in "cushion" lets it sit for hours on hard tree branches.

The koala's rump is like having a portable pillow.

Koalas have pear-shaped bodies that provide them with good balance for perching on tree limbs. They are rather short and stubby, but they have long, powerful arms and legs. These give them the strength they need for climbing.

Koalas have great coordination as they leap from branch to branch. Koalas would make great Olympic gymnasts!

A koala has 2 thumbs and 3 fingers on each of its front paws. The extra thumb is a terrific tool for pulling and grasping leaves. Like cats, koalas need claws to climb. Sharp, curved claws on their front paws help them grip the smooth, hard bark of the eucalyptus tree.

Koalas have 5 toes on each of their back paws. Except for their first toe, their back paws also have claws. The first toe works like a thumb to hold onto things. The second and third toes are joined together. Koalas can use these connected toes to scratch an itch or to comb their fur. The fourth and fifth toes on their feet are used for climbing.

Under all that long hair are the koala's ears, which are very good at hearing many sounds.

Climbing is easy for koalas. First they dig their front claws into the bark of the eucalyptus tree for a strong hold. Then they push them-selves upward with their back paws, and grab the tree again with their front claws.

They almost appear to be hopping up the tree. The pads on the bottom of their front and back paws prevent them from slipping and falling.

Sharp claws help koalas hold onto a branch, even a very skinny one.

Koalas must always keep a tight grip. This is important because koalas climb very high into these trees, often 150 feet!

That's like a person taking an elevator ride to the fifteenth floor of a building.

They climb so high for two reasons: to be safe and to have plenty of fresh eucalyptus leaves to eat.

When a koala finds a good feeding place, it stops and throws an arm or a leg around a tree limb. It will then wedge its body in between the leafy eucalyptus branches. What a nice setting for a snack and a snooze!

In fact, koalas often become so comfortable in these temporary tree houses they may fall asleep while still chewing. Koalas have been spotted sound asleep with half-eaten eucalyptus leaves hanging from their mouths.

Don't worry, this sleeping koala won't fall out of the tree.

Unlike people, they can sleep while sitting up in a tree—and not fall out. They like sleeping as much as eating. Koalas can nap curled up in a tight ball or loosely draped over branches with their arms and legs hanging down.

They usually stay in the same tree for several days at a time, because moving to another tree is a big job. They must carefully climb backward and retrace their steps all the way to the ground. Then they carefully scoot over to a nearby tree and climb high to reach their next meal.

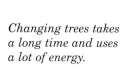

Changing trees takes a long time and uses a lot of energy.

Tree-dwelling creatures like the koalas are arboreal (ar-BOR-ee-ul), which means they prefer to live high above the ground. Koalas consume only leaves, grasses, and other plants, meaning they are herbivores.

Koalas prefer one type of food. They just love to eat eucalyptus leaves. Some people have a favorite food—like pizza, for example. But they normally do not eat it at every meal!

A koala consumes about 1-1/2 pounds of eucalyptus leaves each day. That's an awful lot for its size. Like squirrels, koalas can store food in their cheeks to save for later. This comes in handy when they are hungry and want a quick snack.

Koalas also eat the stems and bark of eucalyptus trees.

Koalas have strong arms and legs because sometimes it's a big stretch to reach the next tree limb.

Eucalyptus trees are also called gum trees. They are evergreens, which means they keep their green leaves year-round.

But that doesn't mean they can grow chewing gum! Eucalyptus "gum" is the sticky sap that oozes through the tree's bark.

Koalas also like to nibble on the stems, flowers, and bark of the eucalyptus tree. In addition to furnishing koalas with food, these trees provide protection from rain, and shade them from the hot Australian sun.

Eucalyptus leaves are poisonous to most animals. But koalas have special stomachs that can process the tree's oils. Once digested, these strong-scented oils help repel blood-sucking fleas and lice.

The oils also give koalas a sweet eucalyptus scent. Some people say they smell like a refreshing eucalyptus cough drop!

Pages 26 and 27: The Australian sun can be very hot, so koalas keep cool in the shade of eucalyptus trees.

Koalas have powerful jaws equipped with 30 teeth for chewing. Their scissor-sharp front teeth help them shred the tough eucalyptus leaves. Flat back teeth enable them to grind and mash their meal before swallowing it.

There are about 600 varieties of eucalyptus. But koalas are picky eaters. Scientists estimate that they will only choose to eat between 20 and 30 of them.

Koalas can locate the leaf types they like best just by sniffing the trunks of the eucalyptus trees. The koala's smooth black nose is covered with hundreds of tiny hairs. These special hairs make it especially sensitive to smells.

Once a koala finds a kind of eucalyptus it likes, it will eat and eat and eat.

Like most nocturnal animals, koalas do not have very strong eyesight. They rely more on their superb senses of smell and hearing to warn them of approaching danger. They must be aware of eagles that can swoop down and snatch their babies.

And even though koalas can trot or gallop, they must also always beware of land predators. The biggest threat is the reddish brown wild Australian dog called the dingo. The small koala is defenseless against this powerful hunter. So koalas must avoid dingoes while traveling on land.

If necessary for an escape, koalas are good swimmers too. But if they smell trouble, they will always climb up the closest tree. That is where they are safest.

Koalas can detect danger by using their excellent senses of smell and hearing.

Being nocturnal, koalas become more active after dark than during daylight. But like children, koalas can't stay up all night. Most people sleep about 8 hours each day. During a typical day, koalas sleep between 18 and 22 hours.

Some people think koalas are lazy because they sleep so much. Or because they seem to move in slow motion. They definitely don't appear to be in a hurry! And there is a very good reason. Eucalyptus leaves are low in nutrients (NU-tree-ents). Even though koalas eat a lot of them, the leaves don't provide them with much energy. So koalas must conserve their energy by moving slowly and getting plenty of sleep.

Sleeping at least 18 hours a day helps koalas conserve energy.

Unlike most mammals, koalas never make dens or permanent homes. They do have home territories, but they will not stay in one particular tree.

Also, koalas like to be alone. Several koalas may live in the same area, but they will not socialize (SO-shul-ize), or hang out together. If more than one ends up in the same tree, they will avoid each other and stay on separate branches.

Koalas spend time with each other only when they are ready to mate or when a mother is raising her baby.

This koala mother is teaching her baby to climb safely.

One male will usually share his home territory of about 15 different trees with up to 6 females.

He will mark his territory by rubbing a scent gland on the center of his chest against the bottoms of his trees. The odor is an invisible message. It warns other males that they are not welcome in his area.

Koalas are usually quiet, but they can be very noisy if they have something to say.

Koalas also communicate by making noises, which include growling, grunting, groaning, and whining. When the males want to attract a mate, they sit on their rumps, lift their snouts skyward, and roar.

Scientists report that the male's courting call sounds more like a ferocious beast than a mild-mannered koala.

Males can begin breeding after they turn 3 years old. Females usually can breed by age 2.

On average, female koalas reproduce about once every other year. They have one baby, called a joey, at a time. Twins are extremely rare. Males and females will always go their separate ways after mating. The female koala raises the baby by herself.

Baby koalas are born pink, bald, blind, and about the size of a jelly bean. A newborn koala must immediately crawl into its mother's pouch. This journey is very difficult and usually takes about 5 minutes.

Once inside the pouch, the joey begins feeding on its mother's milk. Even though the pouch opens upside down, the tiny koala can't fall out. A muscle at the bottom of the pouch tightens to keep the baby inside. While her joey is safe and snug in her pouch, the mother koala can continue life as normal.

This young joey is tightly holding onto its mother's fur.

At around 6 months old, the baby pops its furry face out for its first peek at the world.

The joey now looks like a miniature version of its mother. It communicates to her in high-pitched squeaks.

By this time the joey begins to want more to eat than just milk.

Mother koalas do a good job of protecting their young joeys.

So the mother gives her baby a food called pap, which is partly digested eucalyptus leaves that she has pre-chewed. The baby likes this new food. Pap gives the joey a little taste of eucalyptus and prepares its stomach for digesting solid leaves.

By 8 months old, a joey can pull itself out of the pouch. The joey clings to its mother's belly as she climbs through the trees. If it feels frightened or tired, it can always go back into the pouch. As it grows bigger and braver, the koala baby begins riding piggyback or on top of its mother's head.

By 12 months old, the joey wants to eat only eucalyptus leaves. No more mother's milk and no more pap. The mother koala begins teaching her baby which eucalyptus leaves are good to eat.

At about 18 months, the young koala is now ready to leave its mother and live alone. It will find a territory of its own.

Koalas are not really fully grown until they turn 4 years old. Scientists say koalas in the wild usually live between 10 and 14 years.

Koalas spend most of their lives high up in trees.

People of all ages seem to like koalas. Yet humans have been the biggest threat to their survival. There was a time when koalas almost disappeared completely. That was long ago, when people shot them for sport and to sell their coats. Since 1927 Australia has had laws that protect koalas from being killed.

But the places where they live are not protected. Today the major threat to koalas is the loss of their habitat. As cities expand into their eucalyptus forests and replace trees with buildings, many koalas lose their homes. Some koalas have been seen in dangerous traffic areas. And they have been killed by motorists who do not expect them to be there.

The safest place for a young koala is riding piggyback on its mother.

Loss of habitat continues to force koalas into other human environments.

They have been spotted perched on fences and on street signs. They have climbed up telephone poles. These koalas are lost and scared. Fortunately, there are people who are trying to help them.

With our help, koalas will continue to live in their original wild habitats.

Many koalas are rescued and taken to parks and preserves. These protected areas are sanctuaries (SANK-chu-air-ees), or safe places, for them to live. Some of these sanctuaries have hospitals that treat injured koalas and then return them to their original habitats. Others provide them with permanent homes.

The koala is a threatened species. Some scientists estimate that there are about 40,000 to 80,000 koalas left in the wild. And although the koala still faces many challenges to its future, the Australian government and people who care about koalas are helping to protect them.

GLOSSARY

Aborigines: People who are native to a region, especially Australia (page 6).

Arboreal: Living in or frequenting trees (page 22).

Camouflage: Markings or coloration that help an animal blend in with its surroundings to hide it from enemies (page 9).

Habitat: A place in nature where an animal or plant lives (pages 44, 46, 47).

Herbivores: Animals that eat plants (page 22).

Mammals: Vertebrates (animals with backbones) whose females produce milk to feed their young (pages 5, 35).

Marsupial: A mammal, such as the koala and kangaroo, that carries its young in the mother's pouch (page 5).

Nocturnal: Active at night (pages 6, 31, 32).

Nutrient: A nourishing ingredient in food (page 32).

MORE BOOKS TO READ

Endangered Animals of the Southern Continents. In Peril (series) by Barbara J. Behm and Jean-Christophe Balouet (Gareth Stevens)

Koala by Caroline Arnold (Morrow)

A Koala is Not a Bear by Hannelore Sotzek and Bobbie Kalman (Crabtree)

Why Mammals Have Fur by Dorothy Hinshaw Patent (Dutton)

VIDEOS

Australia (Walt Disney Home Video)

Koalas (Film Ideas, Inc.)

Koalas: The Bear Facts (Bullfrog Films)

WEB SITES

www.koala.net.au/

ww.koalarescue.npf.org/au/koala5.html

Some web sites stay current longer than others. For further web sites, use your search engines to locate the following topics: *aborigines, eucalyptus, joeys, koalas, mammals, marsupials,* and *wildlife of Australia.*